# Listening to the Leaves Form

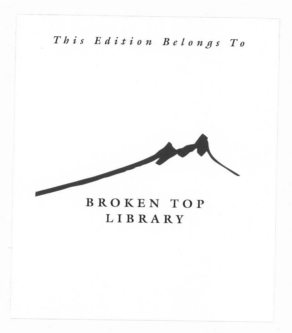

## Other Books by James Grabill

*Poem Rising Out of the Earth and Standing Up In Someone*

*Through the Green Fire*

*In the Coiled Light*

*To Other Beings*

*One River*

*Clouds Blowing Away*

# *Listening*

## *to the*

# *Leaves Form*

## Poems

### *by*

## James
## Grabill

Lynx House Press
Portland, Oregon / Amherst, Massachusetts

## ACKNOWLEDGMENTS

Grateful acknowledgment is made to editors of the following publications where some of the poems in this book first appeared: *Atomic Ghost*, an anthology from Coffee House Press ("Dream of the Closeness of Venus"), *Barnabe Mountain Review* ("A Dream of the Horse"), *Calapooya Collage* ("Light Entering the World" and "Ode to the Soup"), *Fine Madness* ("Uncle Cindy's Prosperity Driving Down the Road," "Wilbur Turning Off the Alarm-Radio," and "On the Brink of Aluminum"—"On the Brink of Aluminum" was nominated by the editors for a Pushcart Prize), *Fireweed* ("A Spark That Keeps Flying," "In Praise of the Trees This Fall," "Shower," and "All This Is Modified"), *Germination* ("Onion"), *The Greenfield Review* ("Report of the Fuel"), *Ground Water Review* ("Living Near the Marsh"), *High Plains Literary Review* ("The Next Light"), *Hubbub* ("Two Rusty Quarters" and "After One of the Dreams"), *The Kerf* ("Ochre Sea Stars on the Shore Rocks" and "A Report of the Immensity"), *Mentor* ("Mid-Life"), *Mid-American Review* ("The Finches"), *Mythos Journal* ("Sandbagging the Banks"), *Poetry East* ("Some Transmutation of Desire: A Momentum"), *The Prose Poem* ("A Report on How It's Gotta Be Hard"), *Rain City Review* ("Rooms Lit from the Reaches"), *Raven Chronicles* ("The OCA Isn't a Bunch of Grackles"), *The Seattle Review* ("Postcard of the Luminous Dark Red Ocean Fish"), *Silverfish Review* ("Some of These Things" and "In the Sanctuary of Forgetting"), *South Dakota Review* ("On the Beach in Heavy Wind at the Edge of a Grain of Sand"), *The Stone Drum* ("Flash of a Dragonfly"), *Willamette Week* ("The Sound of the Door Closing"), and *Willow Springs* ("As It Rains," "With the Jade," "Staying Alive," "Working with Desire," and "The Unanswering Will Go Unanswering").

Library of Congress Cataloging-in-Publication Data

Grabill, James, 1949-
        Listening to the leaves form : poems / James Grabill.
           p. cm.
        ISBN 0-89924-097-6 (Cloth) —— ISBN 0-89924-096-8 (pbk.)
        I. Title.
    PS3557.R115L57 1997
    811'.54--dc21                                    97-16189
                                                   CIP

Lynx House Press books are distributed by
Small Press Distribution, 1814 San Pablo Avenue, Berkeley, CA 94702

Lynx House Press
9305 SE Salmon Ct.
Portland, OR 97216

and

Box 640
Amherst, MA 01002

Printed in Canada

I wish to extend special thanks to editor Christopher Howell for his collaborative assistance and insights, and to editors, teachers, and friends Dan Raphael, George Kalamaras, John Bradley, Bill Tremblay, Leiv Kadmon, Wendy Davis, Diane Averill, John Benson, David Mount, Jeff Knorr, Barbara LaMorticella, James Tipton, and Thomas R. Smith for their deep-currented correspondence and camaraderie. This book is dedicated to these fine people, to my companion Marilyn Burki, to my family, and to the Family of the Arts.

---

There is, all around us,
this country
of original fire.

You know what I mean.

—Mary Oliver

# CONTENTS

## III.  *Living Near the Marsh*

# I.

# On the Brink of Aluminum

The core of every core, the kernel of every kernel,
an almond! Held in itself, deepening in sweetness:
all of this, everything, right up to the stars,
is the meat around your stone. . . .

. . . something has already started to live
in you that will live longer than the suns.

—R.M. Rilke

# SOME OF THESE THINGS

You've got the lull and expanse, coves, listening through drawings in caves, each contour . . . a grosbeak, or a spoon, or table, and the Ford and floor. It's all in the light making the plants.

Or maple artery, green unborn, flicker feathers, bread of the light, the plant masks, the asking. You've got the Saturday pollen, and parting, calling. Or the weathermen and coyotes and diggers and yeomen and beats and jives and rigs and laces and bowls and oranges. You've got the small hole of the tear, ebony floors in the sweep of a second hand, the hold of a shoulder.

Or room vistas, the falling blue, horse seaweed dripping from old chorus lines, sunrises off to the left, fleecy road love, a mystic's shadow, the hard muscle of the tear. It's in the Hindu breathing rocks, the grasslit August lips, the sun's feathers, the bicycle crate, the buttressed helium, the naked candle. Where it's thought out of itself, the only time it will happen. Where it's in the listening mint scent. You've got the only time it will happen.

Or morning skin. Centers of curry. First cinnamon. Underground trees and rain under the ground of that, and skin under the ground of that, and night under that, and over. And through stratospheres of guitars. In folds of the oats. You've got it in your necklace of fire. You've got it in your rain through the leaves.

# A RED LEAF

A leaf bursts from its spool.
Already it is red with heat.
Already it is smooth
as a basset hound's velvet ear.
Basements steaming with minerals
hover offshore of the small houses.
The plasma of enforced mistakes
echoes irregularly.
The composing helix
of flying off red coals.
The lunar pointillism
of a score of night skies
seen together overhead.
The constant needs
of each particle
of attention attended to.
The magnetics
of vulnerable solidness.
The scent of tenderness.
One finds herself here.
In a cafe we did not say.
A horse's run past the earth
with its trees lit and full.
The bread locked in a history.
The God in an emotion.
Already the motors cooling
on their knees.
Already the leaf
lit from before
anything is seen.

# LIGHT ENTERING THE WORLD

The shapes of light are concaved strata in plumbings of vegetables and markings on turtles. The plateaus of wheat sway under a wind from someone's back turned at work, facing the terminal where computations flicker in star countries of our names, where numbers allocated in projections of themselves that are solid and shaped, and kept on shelves, create sound we hear from or pick up soul work that has been coming down.

So the light is moth wings flickering all over a field where night soaks in a punchpress snap of a twig or slip of a strap down a shoulder, the dew-soaked lines sliding and wet and the grass thick and cool. And light is what caring about the end of the war did to the glistening belt buckles, to the dust behind automobiles swirling invisibly blue-black with radio molten asking what happened when that person had to have been thinking to have done that.

A turtle the size of a table walks up to remind us about—what's she saying? You want to hold her, but you can't. She is too wide, too much a table diving down into the waves of light of what is assumed. You can't follow her—her thin vulnerable neck and hairless head, her rugged face still with you in the light. Her shell is textured intricately in colors of the earth and sky, in symbols, but what do they look like? What would a symphony made from them sound like? Where did the turtle swim, with part of this city in late afternoon around her, leaving behind this part of the hour?

# TWO RUSTY QUARTERS

(a report of feeling at a loss)

In their calls, wild birds know the prism, the sunlight split into things. They know the angle of a red streaking insect. A week is a month. One bird will come back for another, or leave.

After things have been forgotten, they appear. Downtown a man calls you brother and asks for "two rusty quarters." The changing light between buildings builds its temple in the amber haze. You might give your brother your car, beneath the sun's first world, if it would do the right good.

But nobody's up to it. The brother is angry, grimy. The knife on his belt is close to his hand. You can't look at him. We're driving the cars we can't control and have to go to work. As fragments hover in nests of desire. As being late might harbor some rusted fire stairs and bed springs behind the name of a place. As the face on TV flies through the air.

Is the car going to make it sometimes you wonder. A man not far from the open window, asking for two rusty quarters, is a brother, and yet the rain in his face is wine prisming the place he sees. A quarter will turn to red, as a bird answers the ground by flying, as a clerk in front of the old grocery hits the sidewalk with a hard spray of water from a garden hose. The car needs gas, and work.

How rare to be given a body. How much earth is in a quarter's wine? When birds fly, cars rush through the light. Men wake up into their old blankets and coats. How much could go wrong, and how much more? Everything flies through the prism, dividing up the world, and we don't know what to do.

# AS IT RAINS

I've struggled with the slides
and the benefits withheld
or given, realizing the blue light
doesn't care about money or punching
the clock in or out. It is democratic
and anarchist, ancient, like the sky,
reminding us to see its blue and its light
as part of our blue and our light.
And as it waits, flowing, only itself,
maybe the world is a waterfall
and likewise our bodies. Perhaps
everything we see as steady
and balanced is part of the waterfall.
Every speech and announcement,
every address and graded test,
every book, and every workweek
is falling, energetic, in gravity,
in sunlight, darkness, the months
it takes, in cries of babies,
in ocean coast rumbling, releasing,
in blue jays who respond.
And every grain of salt is falling
in a waterfall of sun and earth
and people's voices and business
deductions and squirrel work
and hazelnuts forming. All things
we own are falling in a waterfall
spent by ancestors, locomotions
of wealth in the tiniest spaces,
in the belt buckle broken off
from marriage and freedom,
in a shoe lace untied on a boy's foot
in August, and the mastodons
are falling in the waterfall
of moss growing and the cities
are falling in the scent

of white blossoms, releasing,
reverberating, the coast
of their falling, the waterfall
of weeks, the wild cats in Colorado
foothills, everything asked for
and everything found, the spume
of forgetting and remembering,
the chopped onions on the counter.
And still the blue and the light
wait, the blue light entirely
itself, radiant, quiet,
from before all thought.

# ODE TO THE SOUP

(the soul is everywhere, full of everything)

If you start with vegetable bouillon mixed in hot water and add slices of celery, cross-sections of carrot, methodically soaked black beans, and add tofu fried in sesame oil, fronds of broccoli and heart stem, cerebral sections of cauliflower, along with spontaneously diced ceilings of green pepper cathedrals, and you boil them with the brown rice no one ate the night before, and with zucchini that was fried in the sesame, and you add a hundred astrological onion curves with a clove of garlic for each person who will be eating, and you cook it, adding futuristic green beans and pea pods, parsley and broken bread, and you set the crock pot on its forward momentum, you begin to get soup.

You might add grated tofu cheese or cheddar, you might add a few hours when the house seemed to be silent, or the pintos that were soaked a few days before, or the barley from a friend's speech, or the yellow pepper still sweet from its asking, and you might add sea salt, black pepper from a mill, freshly dried herbs from what has been happening, and the soup will grow.

The heat that the wires make in the crock pot leans back into its impulses, and rests on the river water driving its turbines, on the people working there back in the canyon, and the heat comes from inside the workweek where the money was constructed out of its sticks and mud, where the body was given over to regulations, where the mind was entirely its cauliflower of utility. This energetic damming up of the properties rain has been falling through, of the breath that ground has carried in its minerals, in the calcium of bones lit at night by ancestral charges, in the salt whose mirrors show through one room to another, one face to another, this holding back of the power we are capable of, that channels through the roots of the house and heats the water, invests what it has hoped as it lingers for hours, cooking the soup.

People we have never seen, hands that picked the vegetables, sea lions that swam in the water, machines that stamped out the bouillon, scrubbers that assembled the tomatoes, ministers who sailed in on the garlic, traffic that bent down over the salt mines, pepper in the old hotels that were forgetting, red Wyoming in the viscous expenses, newscasters teleported through the kernels of grain, musicians whose celery strings were tuned to a pitch of human legs, football tenements lounging in the apex of dried leaves, white mustard barricading its bay scent with carrot sweat, warehouses of the potatoes added later, and the Victorian bacteriological purposes of shape and structure bathe in the soup.

The soup is electromagnetic with nearby pines, with the gardens gone down into their yield, with the arms seen from windows of buses, with umbrellas hovered over an hour of indecision, and it bubbles with planetary froth, cooks in the wake of recessions, and heats up the air in the kitchen with its women's and men's names, with its porches where a door can be opened, with hunger that will know what it accomplishes, with its sexual waters that spread from the radio passing through it. Dusk also passes through, and ocean rumbling from 80 miles off, and the drawers opened after a shower, and ships plunging through their visuals.

Floridian pavilions lionize the basil, sit-coms gather in the spoked elevators of canicular membranes, flakes of oxidized expedium break from vaporous folds, and the voices of restaurants threaded through with savory drape the windows of implied finger lifts. The cheekbones of cauliflower mix with guitar lightning of garlic played at half-blues deep in the heat that bowls ask out of. Faces appear in our faces, bones in our bones, herbal forests in our heat, as the soup is stirred, as the aromatic marjoram concocts its breast heat, as the meat left out brings in its lockers, as the taxis discard their backseats into the broth of centuries, as the bagpipers march from the ancient hill into the city.

The caldron is stirred, the heat of the molecules glistens, the trombones slide through the onions in the cathedral, the raccoon tantrums broker the barley sanctions, the hotel room plows through the nectarine celery, the long distance phone calls come in down the hoops of carrot cells, through the turbulence of primordial witch coals, through the dog hunts lost in the apocrypha, through the vulgate circles of designs on ties that the insurance pressure demands of its teenaged math classes, that the man whose body is naked asks of the air.

There is a mother of broccoli eating up the horsetails, a willow whose weather has been crying under the red nails, an oak lost in the squash, an icon given over to water, a photograph of the way it ought to be, boiled up from the mud of cross-disciplinary tomatoes. The soup is cooked, given a second on earth, given a flash of conscious beginning, and the genetic countryside glows for miles from the window of the car. The house floats down a Nile of preconditions. The owl whose voice became a quartz crystal channels the nature of the air. There is soup steaming at each instance of the cosmos, at each vernacular moth wind turning, in each cosmetic preponderance of desire.

The way big cats moan goes down in the onions, desire of the silky legs and retreat of the asparagus go down, with the heat of the old cultures of potatoes, with the shields melted down from distant speeds. European espresso goes down, and mint on the lips of the evangelist, and illuvial pipes played up from the lungs of farm animals, and the grit of singed fortunes that a hand signed off when it took on its glow. There are meeting rooms stewing, distant luxuries bleeding, courageous cataclysms honored in the smoke of the red-brown spider eggs of heat, in the feathery moss on the Oregon trees that lean into the wealth.

The soup cooks through the weekend, and through the lives of neighbors, and through the lines on the face of the tortoise. It rounds out through the harbors of sudden knowledge, and asks for its cultural espionage in the wings of a nut scent. It commands great armies of tomato cells and drives through mountainous water with its urging and fortune-telling back in the string beans of our ribs, in the cauliflower testes that wander, in the mystery of the carrot and the dried lotus pod carted through the January of nations and leaves.

We stir the soup with our breathing, with our imagery of health, and it roils in underground cooking. The soup enters the way a bowl sits on the table, the way the table stands on its stone, the way the umbrella of progress lines up with the curving caldron, the way words dive into their broth and are part of us.

# ONION

So the day wraps around the earth,
>    and night wraps around its day,
>    and distance wraps around the mind
>    and its tiniest thing.

So months stand up around us,
>    flaming in fuels
>    of the vegetables,
>    in a eucalyptus grove,
>    in the scent of rain.

So walls cover the light of sleep,
>    and a breath covers the trees
>    in our chests, and day wraps
>    around with its oceans.

So winds cover their ground,
>    and roads uproot the villages,
>    and events recover our lives,
>    and blue jays appear and vanish,
>    and the soup lifts into its warmth
>    and is taken.

# POSTCARD OF THE LUMINOUS DARK-RED OCEAN FISH

Blue sky, after weeks of rain.  The knotted grind of a distant mower, and another.  When they stop, a finch is singing.  And another.

I look at the postcard of the ocean fish staring into the camera with her or his huge dark-red face.  The body like a microscopic piece of primordial blood, one of the cells diving near the bottom of the brain, carrying some lit air and a few magnesium spins of memory, maybe something about Akron.

I'm back, in awe, listening to the wild finch, thinking of the way movement made eyes, the way rhythms made feathers and fins, the way questions took on shoulders.

Walking in one direction, is it anywhere, without the regard we are capable of?  In my house, I am secure, in the breathing house.  Still, my regard flies out, asking, longing . . . for you? . . .

I look back at the red fish whose species someone named "Irish Lord," her or his oval eyes, the seven fins and ocean crusts without question.  Answers around me flare up in fins, without clear questions.  The answers say this is the one hour and all is here.  In the new day, this is the one hour, and all is here.

# IN THE OPEN HOUR

for Doug

It wakes in the eco-matrix of the forest scent of snow
and in how the absent New York theater of pinecones
meeting again on the ground speaks out its blue flames
around the mountain tree, in a halo that our music reaches
by giving itself to its unthought chords, and new islands

we bodily feel approaching, the summer lightning DNA
latched to its immense star-spiralled sun unhooked from days,
then back. I want to unknow it, to then find the ocean
blossoming backyard tree as the snow falls home again
into its arms, to see the birds in a feather of gas or stone,

or down brick-paved avenues painters connect through shelled
second floor tides rising into the bay of their paints
leaving a brush, through healing flames of pine trunks,
a dog-brown of the elken yard from 1954 afternoon blue sky
past all invisible thought, stream-veined cars flooding

the streets in molten metal rumbling that light rides
as on volcanic waves off Oregon, the winter apple scent
threading the uncle's artery with the balloon catheter,
or slam of a steel drum down onto the pier an hour invents,
through reverse funnels of light opening, breathing,

the ocean waves breaking petals out to their first home
as they form, that a dragonfly touches with its Celtic body
from a past no longer waiting for anything, but around us
it forgets us, as we enter an hour of another person
entering an hour of another, on and on . . .

# THE O.C.A. ISN'T A BUNCH OF GRACKLES

(a prose poem of protest)

I've wanted to write about the grackles that nest in the branches and on the roof near our upstairs windows. I used to think they were birds of noise, that they didn't know how to sing. I never spent time with them like this, so close to their nests, listening to their long down-floating whistles softly in wind, their screeing about how the air picked them up into drafts, and calming each other down in primal coos. I hear them talking about where the corn is, and the water. A few of their songs are elegant.

I say this in the face of the OCA as they mercilessly campaign against human rights. I am looking for the door that will show how their words weren't what we thought. I know they are talking about something else, certainly not men and women alive in the world with as much right to their lives as anyone. I know I shiver when the OCA prays.

There is no comparison between grackles and the contemptuous noise of some people. I feel sick I brought the grackles into this poem but will leave them in because I like them a lot now. I feel their strength. A few of their songs come from inside the trees.

---

(Note: The OCA, or Oregon Citizens' Alliance, is an organization that vigorously fights to limit legal protections for those unlike themselves.)

24

# AFTER ONE OF THE DREAMS

The green '58 Pontiac swerves around the corner, a sleeping old man driving. It slides to a stop in front of a large wooden house vanishing as he wakes.

A woman who knew him beautifully was inside that house. A woman he loved wholly.

Apple scent drifts from nearby solidness.

He looks at the tree, full of rain from the ocean. A rain from sea lions and iridescent squid. A rain from plants still beneath the day, and from people's backs, from Japan's steaming docks.

With walnut bread and French roast, he sits in the morning, touching her far away as he hears the rain.

The rain is a wave unfolding.

A man who learns to love beyond his call to another is inside him, becoming him.

The slow rain is falling in distant canyons, before he was here. And after.

# THE FINCHES

Sunflower seeds in the tray and spilled over the ground call to the trees, to the eyes in the trees. Burning deeply violet into themselves, the sunflower seeds call.

I chase away the young cat, and go back into the house. At first, a finch swoops to a lower branch, then more, then finches are in the branches and on the power lines, in split seconds, landing by the seeds, taking them into their tiny beaks and cracking them, turning them over and pressing their tongues into them.

A reddened male sings wildly from the eaves, and some fly exactly into places where others are, as if they could exchange bodies, and many walk over and over the warm seeds on the ground.

The air is full of sunlight and violet shadows streaming from our bodies, in this place the seeds burn open, where words become seeds, and small things at work, and the sounds of the car become seeds, or the shape of the chairs, or the friend's voice over the phone, or the green soup cooling.

# ON THE BRINK OF ALUMINUM

Buck knew about aluminum
from the way his paycheck
felt lighter than it looked,

and the way it shined
with names of the company,
with figures and computation.

Even if he worked hard,
his paycheck had this aluminumal
collapse of its substance

into a kind of wrapping
for what he tried to contain
in the form of a place to live

or objects and food and activity.
If his mind wandered, still
the paycheck wavered in its thin

borders of believability.
If his mind focused on it,
the paycheck vibrated and vanished,

reappeared and vanished, the squids
jetting through dark-red arenas
after the country is flooded

by miles of seawater—sturgeon
hovering in the horse stalls.
A herd of wild tuna ranging over

glistening modernist warehouses
of some hungers.  Opalescent jellyfish
parachuting elegantly, sideways

through open mirrors of kitchen
supplies, like something escaped
from people's chests, in the sheen

of cooking pots, the sink
translucent, and shelves jammed
with abalone and mussels who wove

their steel veins together
into a ground they make up.
Buck looked back at the paycheck,

which had now become 20s and 50s
showing a Many-Ribbed Hydromedusa
in the silver Pacific evening

in the oval in the middle, her mare
tails shivering under her dome,
over the ocean floor's sanctuary.

Buck thought about the green anemone
crowding in caverns at work,
and some of the floors disguised

in swirled-up mud.  He knew where
old rockfish burrow in amniotic murk,
near barnacles latched onto the bell

of a tuba, the eels glaring
from the electrical dark
of unfelt concern.  Aluminum

was the opposite of the bottom fish,
bonefish, thundered into soil
by tons of amoebic slownesses,

suspended infra-radiant in ocean
contents of the computer waters.
Aluminum in the country of paychecks

was an ancestor of how things breathe,
flattened into foil mostly,
and sold to everyone possible.

Aluminum in the way light fell
was a glint and tingling, like
a fear of radio waves passing

through the skin of your only body
as you live in the 20th century.
Buck tried to forget the ocean,

and suddenly could see
21st century aluminum
like a hologram of itself,

around what it wants to hold
or cover up, and paychecks
also this other substance,

and steaming fallen redwoods
flattened into some kind of foil
you could unroll to see the land.

# ON THE BEACH IN HEAVY WIND
# AT THE EDGE OF A GRAIN OF SAND

In the sand the wind rushes
toward its cliff, the oniony slivers
glisten between roof grains

of sediments, bellicose grindings,
shreds of sea lion, stewed amorphic
scaffolding, housings half buried

by thundering, yet flowing
the river of sand on the floor
of the wind, mushroom skulls

cracked into flakes of bowl-like
sounds from fifth grade, spears
of salmon bones translucent,

thinner than hair when they puncture
the crab's armor-strewn vacant miles
behind the gulls who know what happened.

The torch of some broken appliances
fills a speck with a steely hush
of Phnom Penh, peppered with mango

shavings whose distant islands
saw the pelican lift higher, then
dive into a wave, the seeds vibrating

into the blue, the wave carried
by what it knows. Wind rushes
toward its cliff at the edge

of each grain. Leavings crumble
in the blast of the sun. Moonlight
of the wind hollows the faint membranes

of turtle bone further and steams
in the grasses, snapping tiniest
feathers into their salt, the wind

overflowing with flakes from black
threads of underwater robes, ancient
Klamath anklets ground in a billion

billion times their number of grains
blown and rushing rhythmically
across this young Pacific beach.

# THE SOUND OF THE DOOR CLOSING

It could be in a rush of wind
and branches swaying one evening.
It could be in a tiny click
and release of some kind of hold.
It could be in seeing an old Chevy
by the highway abandoned, certainly
not going anywhere, and a man
climbing into it one evening.
The door closing might sound
like master switches thrown off
at the control panel by engineers
on their way out at 6:00 p.m.,
or look like a woman painting her nails,
the dusk moving almost imperceptibly
through the heavy neighborhood trees.
The door closing might be secret,
then, inside a suit of clothes.
It might hover in the air
for weeks, months, the door
closing, the frontier of the door
taking both sides out of the argument.
Perhaps we should build a great wall
so the door closing won't surprise
anyone. We could invent a philosophy
of the great wall to explain the door
and how it opens, but then closes.
There could be names for the door closing
that carry some of our weight,
the sadness of the closing,
the shock, or sometimes the relief
of the door turning on its axles
and wheeling into its frame.
There is the quiet, finally,
of highway noises blocked out,
the hallway allowed to be itself
without the encumbrance of the room,

the freedom given to another
by just letting the doors go
sometimes into their frames—
all these have their particular
sounds of the trees growing.
So why is it so difficult to get used to?

# II.

# What Will Hold?

I found the land which matched my interior
landscape. The door separating inside and
outside opened. What my eyes saw meshed with
images I carried inside my body. Pictures
painted on the walls of my womb began to emerge.

—Meinrad Craighead

# A DREAM OF THE CLOSENESS OF VENUS

(a report)

### I.

We return to the apartment
in the Colorado mountain town.
The front door swings open.
All the doorknobs, especially
crystal ones, had to be chopped off,
a man tells us, in case
they become radiated.

I look out the window at Seattle
and see the beginning
of intense light, so quickly
Marilyn and I, with the child
we have with us, climb
under the bed.

### II.

It is a large wood-framed bed,
100 years old, or 150.
The dust is thick, the scent
of fungusy pine needles.
There is a wooden place
under the bed where we can hide,
so we climb in.

We hold one another
and wait for the nuclear blast.

III.

In a few minutes, nothing happens.
A few more, still nothing.

Suddenly, neighbors are crowding
into our room, talking excitedly.

We are on the flat apartment house roof,
looking at Seattle, and can see the moon
setting in diamond light
at least ten times
brighter than usual.


IV.

Then a woman notices
a second moon rising
in the south, much larger
than the moon.

As we watch, we see it is Venus,
blue and cratered,
without many swirling clouds,
immensely rising over the town,
almost filling half
of the southern sky,
casting blue light
everywhere around us.

Nobody is afraid.
We look at the blue solar light
on tanks and water purification vats
on other roofs, and blue
down on the streets,
blue melting into the trees
and mountain rock,

as the white moon
sets over the distant ocean,
and Venus nearly
touches Earth
from above us.


V.


It isn't Venus
flying down into the world.
It's Earth
merging with everything around us.

It's Venus bringing blue Earth
back to itself,
hovering immensely near us.

Later in the day, I still feel it,
huge in the southern sky.

# WITH THE JADE

In the tuning, Venus appears
as our bodies, and in our habits,
or what we buy, like what shines out
but can never be touched,
and then huge Venus towers
over the earth one night
in a dream, in the south sky
over the mountain town,
and we just watch her blue
immense presence lifting
everything out of everything.

The trailer shudders, gunned
up the hill by a foreman,
by the typists back on call,
when the boss lifts his finger
and the African cuts into jade
changing the way light falls
on East Cherry a few blocks,
the tiny carving, the typing.
And the flute player in Gambia
knows the seabird's floating
teeth in the starlight eating
at the earth-body, eating it
into its shape, and the car drives
its officers over the ground.

The first work stoppages showed
through the castles like bone
scans turned backwards,
into yellow-brown lights
of the open air that was still
meditating itself into breath,
and money in its castles
was exhaling its village
that darkens or lightens

and all the objects holding
solid, the snow falling
and melting into the air
or ground or the river
of what it will be touching.

The light cutting across
a muskrat's bushy head
is the shadowy pulsing
around a person waking
after a night's sleep back
through the person who carries
him, that he makes himself out of,
that he sees the world out of,
that he wishes to give back
to itself, himself, herself,
that she wishes to set free.

The trains, hours, bellies,
throughout his only body
there are pieces he'd give
back to their passage,
through this stopped time
as he waits in each shadow
of the moon or sunlight,
to where earthen light comes
from those that are free,
and those that were never
caught, with those who
stopped the light in its sea
that prays through what
it brings into form.

# A REPORT ON OUR LACK OF OWNERSHIP

You can't have everything, though, I know, we wanted it. You can't have the lightning of grasses that roots fuel with water from rains. You can't have the orangutan's sweeping reach and roar raking through particles of doubt. You can't have the trapped preserve of what you loved without harming it and yourself, though we wanted it. You can't have the volcanic boiling operatic arpeggios of the factory stamping and booming train cars coupling in the imperative that doesn't back down.

You can't have everything, especially what can't be reached of the other genders or other winds we know are rocking small houses in the mountains of last century inside us. You can't have the great mother sitting down in your chair, and you can't have the midnight galaxies of the scent of bread being baked. You can't have the paycheck, even, because it has been traveling out from its inception like an exhaled breath others are already breathing, and you can't have the coins in your pocket or the friend's hand on your shoulder. Even when it is there, already it is so much else. Already it is so far into the new earth of the sun.

Nothing exists except being here now, and you can't have that. Nothing exists but how we approach others, and you can't have that. Nothing is out with the wailing wolf waters and nothing is in the alcoholic slide. Nothing holds the foolish statement in the air, and you can't have the mown alfalfa fields in the summer Ohio evening coolness. You can't have the buildings that walk through our lives or the roads that drive us. You can't have the single-pitched clarity or intuitive reach or the guitar your bones are holding.

You can't have the stone you are standing on, or the root shades of willow branches or the indigo scent after the rain. And everything you wanted, you simply can't have it. Already it is so much else. Already it is so far into the new earth of the sun. Hammer away all your life, but you can't have it.

# SOME TRANSMUTATION OF DESIRE:
## A MOMENTUM

A momentum before acting
A lamp before light is invented
A cosmic bee hive exhaling a peach tree
    and the yarrow in wind near a mushroom
A tongue lapping the mystical thinness
    and how the lettuce is touched
An Andean rocking of pre-Columbian pelvics
    and parachute of bread scent
    floating the kitchen down
A saying of rain-falling wheat
A Texas of the pilgrims backing up to the flower
    and car engines with licheny myelophonic replies
A country plowed up by radio philosophy
A color in the hair the curve of mahogany
A girlfriend of the Pope's earthiness
    near a distant Tibetan damp-tongued dark
A slender bus station held up invisibly
A light caught in the brain of weight
    funded by the brain of light
A Stream Violet with a real altitude
A saying following its foreign-based shouts
    and nearby banked-on skin lotions
    educated very much into one of the days
An act before motion and weight
A premium caught in the ocean's intimate drain
    of grandfather's fattened sunflower
A rain seen in a moment
A conscious nakedness of celery
An almond shaded in its morning shapes
    and African tusk mask behind museum glass
    of an assumed solidness
A surge through the cardinal cinnamon
A camomile as it steps down
    into the candlelit water

# THE FORGOTTEN

for Allen

A man protests and those who benefit
from how things are going ask what's wrong
with the man protesting. A woman has a child
from inside her enjoyment, and voters decide
she knew what she was doing. A raccoon
freezes in the headlights, cars cranking
both ways on the two-lane road, and nobody
can do anything, for it is night and dark,
and nobody is watching anyway. Almost
everyone is inside in front of their screens.
Lights in the houses are on. Children
go to sleep and dream of computer games.
Dogs imagine a maze of walls and commands.
The slow light from the amber leaves
in the streetlight almost goes unnoticed.

**

Newspapers fly past in a fluttering
of leaves. The weeks shift in a run
of months, and the call drifts into silence.
Cars drive by as the voices on TV shuffle
our words. Few books are opened,
and fewer plans change how things go.
The workweek plows through the neighborhood
in these ways, like a hypnotist florist,
like a bone marrow expert driving back
from a hospital, like a secretary
worn out by the perfection of forms
and courtesy. So a person protests,
who can be sure? Was that a dog barking
or was it the radio? Was that a door
or something settling? What was it
your mother said in her letter?
When did you say we'd have some time
at the ocean for our healing?
And what, again, was the wound?

# UNCLE CINDY'S PROSPERITY DRIVING BACK THE ROAD

Prosperity is the process of selection,
and the back of a hand
hurt while passing through a dumpster
is part of its background radio?
Consensus decides when many forget to vote,
but when will the heron fly over the street
where the house sinks its plumbing
back through high school and grade school?
Thus, can roads that shine
with silvery skins of energy
line the pockets of old habit?
With this in mind, Uncle Cindy applied
for the job with the concrete company.
He drove the truck for decades
in his last job as a person.
Uncle could taste the cinnamon
above the east side of the city.
But first Bingo, then the market
with gum, and banjos over his car motor
sounds, back down one of the avenues
that his hungers had laid out for him.
Thus, the road got pretty thin
sometimes, though he was a good guesser;
still, what was it Rose said
about the microwave heating up
the house inside the walls
until the subatomic tunnels
burst into dark flames of submission
and the house never apparently
existed in this century?
You can't plan for everything,
and still there is the pump organ
concert of the willow trees
in the young barn light,
and the cool stand of the stone walls
from behind his birth, still
near part of the road.

# A REPORT ON HOW IT'S GOTTA BE HARD

It's gotta be difficult, being a train station for the transmigration of souls, carrying the next century inside you, finding yourself visited by ancient great aunts and children, looking into the eyes of the dog and seeing something different: the dog's mother's eyes in her eyes, the deep thinking brain, luminous and dark and charged by her birth!

This might get me worried and protective. I'd want to protect the person I carry from prehistoric threats, from bad smoke and the snakes, from loud misgivings and heated-up appliances. It's gotta be tough, sitting comfortably as you slowly explode but hold smoothly, as you want to read the fetus Allende stories, as you walk outside and feel Neruda beside you like a second husband or boyfriend, the earth speaking its grief and joy around you, saying you are part of this bearing, this carrying.

It's gotta get hard pulling on your socks, reaching down to the floor to pick up the dropped onion, like so many women before, so many women with so many babies waking them at 2 a.m., waking them at 5, with lovers having their own thoughts, with houses having their own troubles. And the waiting, the planning, the suspension of the usual, the edge of not knowing, the breaking sunlight through the window, the luxurious Bach through Yo-Yo Ma's cello and intricacies of dried herbs, the listening strands of a friend's hair and the vitamins, the moral imperative, the laying back, the opening, cramping, in suffering pulses, the final extended volcanic passage and exhaustion.

# STAYING ALIVE

A blue jay hopping
beneath the fir
behind the house
is sometimes all I need,
to remember why
I want to stay alive.

       **

I shook the coins, worried
about our future, and dropped
them six times—thunder over thunder,

the shock and fear of changes,
answered by an ancient
Chinese insight: "Reverence
is the foundation of true culture."

       **

Cover my desk
with monotonous papers
and pipe the technical words
of medical procedures
into my ears for hours,
and let the political
maneuvers rip,
and some day
I'm ready to give up.

But if I can see a blue jay
or a nuthatch clearly, or the face of a raccoon
or one of the squirrels, something in me
switches on, as I feel my body
with their bodies and I feel their bodies
with my body, where we long to be.

# WORKING WITH DESIRE

The Tibetan tulku traveling
your neighborhood invisibly
hovers close to you,
whispering, "pick anything,
anything close to you."

Of course, this doesn't
always work, but when it does . . .

                **

Say you have hunger
and desire and that some
has collapsed into emptiness
while some has caught a fire
of the green cedars
and maturing marigolds,

and some has been returned
by people close to you,
but some is smoldering,
unquenched, inside you:

"pick anything close to you"
and take it in without moving,
without touching it, without
closing off your desire.
The room will brighten.

                **

You work out at the health club
and read one of the magazines
while climbing stairs
on a stair machine.

Suddenly there's a photograph
of Kim Novak in her 60s, at home,
with a pet blue jay on her arm.

This photograph exists.
It is so beautiful.

# WILBUR TURNING OFF THE ALARM-RADIO

Wilbur looked at the clock of the boy's face.
Man, does the grass grow when the earth is relaxed!
And the candy waiting for hunger in an old store
glows more carefully than the cover of a book
asking to be loved because its mother was oceanic
and feminine like the rocks in foothills are feminine.
So the candy, creeping up through the daydreams,
flying through the pastures of subatomic physics
slowed down and was solid, glowing on the shelves
not decomposing at the first thought of absolute Angst.
Wilbur heard the cock crows of dawn and then morning,
about 8:46 on Sunday actually, and he was dreaming
of rooster-pitched violins being tuned in the arms
of attentive Japanese girls whose fathers counted
measures the way rocks broke along faults and ridges,
the way land floating like islands was reaching
a music that held it steady, the way Wilbur reached
toward the clock of the violins making a minute,
and held the button like on a blouse of someone
he just met earlier in his sleep, and held conference
in this instant that clearly he was a man in himself
in a bed that carried him between days to other days,
as the grass does grow when the earth is relaxed
and horses sleep regularly in their back forties
of a nation, and so Wilbur broke ranks with ants
and he opened his arms like willow branches in wind,
no, like masts of ships discovered under the sea.
He gathered his hair on his head and around his pubis
and a little under his arms where someone was cradled,
his whole body vibrating, where someone was touching
him through the air and ground and waters of touching.
This is to say, Wilbur began to wake up and punch down
on the button, and the clock-radio responded by taking
its song down into the unheard waves of the universe.

Wilbur stood up, walked to get his clothing back
from the space around him, and he turned through
the door and stood by the stove, and he simmered,
shimmering, like gold, like atomic waste, he glowed
like children's voices, or like words of grandmothers,
and he so loved his grandmothers, he so loved children
of the neighborhood, and he made coffee to wake a bit more
into the ground of his being here, into the earth dream
that held him here where everyone says we aren't dreaming.

# TWO POEMS ON BEING HERE

I. *An Iris*

Back in, behind the folds,
    an iris light burns
    from the stem of its weathery asking.

In what unfolds, what turns
    through streets, say a quick flash
    from cave walls, blue-violet
    glows in the blue-violet
    of her finding.

In what wildly has been taken
    or was left behind, lightning
    seeds a mountain, crackling
    ultraviolet whiteness viscerally,
    unuseably, beyond freedom.

And the upsurge through a person's body
    as he is alive or she is living
    this life as it is, unlike anything
    else in any other sphere
    of the usual or unfolding—

Heavily did your space ignite
    the Sioux hieroglyphs?

She asked me if I would listen
    from my first birth,
    into the presence of the world.

II. *What Will Hold?*

A mountain in the distance, the heron
    how far we could have felt.

Rhododendron revolving
    in the round
    light of suddenness . . .

When the grass shakes, a dragonfly
    hovers, when the heron's
    eyesight is her own.

It's one person at a time born here.

Like no other, the witness grows,
    always the one who was born.

When everything happens, still
    it is true, an afternoon
    in the body, gulls flying
    in their vastness, the purple
    where the grape will form.

# REPORT ON FIR TREES IN ONEOTA GORGE

We looked at the huge fir trees growing out of the cliff banks in the Oregon gorge, and someone said the trees must be strong, their roots must be immense, to be so calm and solid in this precarious place. And then someone pointed out that it isn't just that, it isn't just that the trees and their roots are strong, but the earth is holding them here. It is the earth that is strong, the massive ground of the earth and rocks holding the roots down. It is the ground that is strong, so the trees grow in these wild places and do not fear for their lives.

And it is the ground that must be strong as we walk through the days and find ourselves in some of the hot wind from people unable to tolerate others not like them. It is ground that takes away anger, that swallows the lightning and rain, that holds our buildings firmly and lets our roots sink into the night world when we sleep, the ground that carries actual dreams in its water.

And it is the ground that is breathing as we are breathing, ground we are made of partly, that holds the fires of the sky inside us, crackling with grasses and vegetables, with proteins of what has been growing and nucleic owl calls and squirrels holding fir trees steadying the cliff, but the ground steadying whatever appears this early in the history of the world.

# A SPARK THAT KEEPS FLYING

When a blue jay breathes,
a spark flies into a mustardy lichen hollow,
and another into a salmonberry's knuckle
and into a seed of long buffalo moss
and another into a cliffrose.

When blue jay breathes
on a moss-haired limb
behind the falls, maple leaves glow,
resonating, with late afternoon in August.

When a blue jay breathes,
a crow near the resinous top
of a Sitka Spruce full of sparks
breathes, over hundreds of uncoiling ferns
in each run the ground makes, the river gorge
towering over small parked cars by the lodge,
and dark-red and black bark beetles scrambling
along the moment they can't be seen.

When a blue jay breathes,
the ferns reach into clear daylight
and hold their shaded greens on the edge
of a spectrum mostly invisible,
though prisming at the rims of water
and wet eyes and juice on thick cedar bark.

And the roots and dense channels of soil
spark with electrical veins in the living
ground, lit from their cells,
where sun and shape are crackling,
pulsing, from inside the sound
of fir needles breathing
in waves for miles and miles.

When a blue jay breathes,
a spark flies into me.
It is still flying
when I lie down in bed
beside Marilyn,
whom I love.

# IN PRAISE OF THE TREES THIS FALL

(after the death
of a friend's father at 80)

The yellow-gold leaves
were wild here for weeks
as if something magnificent were dying.

At the south edge of the city,
forests on each side of the freeway
were radiant, brilliant, as if the road
had meaning, wherever it was going.

And prayers that had no churches
broke out of the tigery bushes—
as if the dark days, too, will be lit,
combusting with root imperative
of words or no words and what is given
freely, without thought of return?

Some of the trees blaze in the fall
because there is nothing more to do.
There is no place other to go.
There is no other world
where we could be more whole
or wholly awake than this place
we were given our lives.

Perhaps that is some of the peace
in the body after a person dies,
that this was the world
we were waiting for, after all?

*This is the world,* the luminous
amber and yellow leaves say,
the edge of light turning and surging
less directly, still less directly—
until this is all there is to be?

Earth-energy burns inside all we are,
and when someone dies,
possibly after much suffering,
the peace is wild, golden,
magnificent, and then given
back to the source forever.

# MID-LIFE

There is only so much space
in the middle of a single thing,

in the swoop of a sea gull
in wild air over the river,

or the classifications of dreams
or purchase of distant retirements.

There are so many rooms in the building,
but only so many, and then the rooms

must come from inside the psyche.
There are so many desires to fulfill,

but then the fulfillment needs, mostly,
to come from inside simply being here.

There are so many lovers, only so many,
and so many houses but only one suddenly.

History charges forward with its billions
of people, so one might linger in a single life,

in the middle of this middle of things
where our goals change into process,

where meaning is often not even doing
but being.  I realize I am missing

valuable photographs that never were taken
about this, and that I seldom can hear

voices of those who will carry us
in their hearts, as the wild air

over the river is with us, and the rooms
where we will live are where we are living.

It is a matter of translation perhaps,
an energy of personage.  It is suddenly hearing

a cry from an unseen pheasant in a park
where hunting has been slowly outgrown.

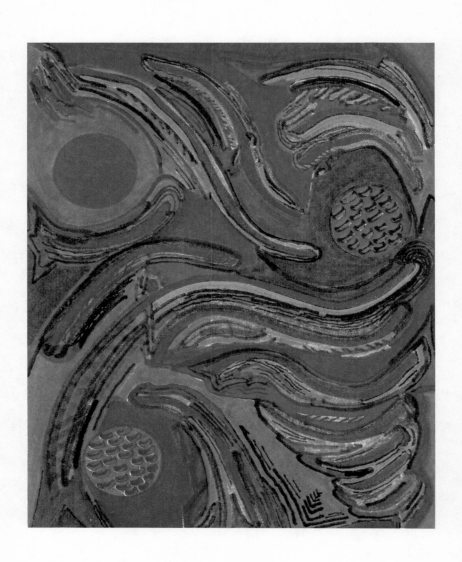

# III.

# Living Near the Marsh

When the heron flies,
Our houses drink
From the ground.

When the heron flies,
We work each day
And sleep in the night.

When the heron flies,
A ladder sleeps
In the grass.

# OCHRE SEA STARS ON THE SHORE ROCKS

Some beings in the cosmos
do not look like photographs
we have of them in our minds.

For instance, the ochre sea stars
look more like men climbing
out of the sea than starfish,

and they have lava in their arms
as they cling like sailors
who drowned but did not die,

who are here, flying through
the rock now steadying themselves
in the stillness before another wave

in the tumult of all waves breaking
over their bodies with the lost
horses and rib cages of light

a grass holds out through the wind,
that the stomach feels, and starfish
know this, and hold the rock

to part of the sky speaking
in a dream, or a person seeing them
is crying behind the thick

ocean bottom of his timeclock,
the primitive rocks calling us,
until we see them in the world.

# A REPORT ON THE IMMENSITY

The ocean waves break and roll, molten with thunder, and ochre sea stars grip on the rock in water churning the raw daylight foaming and surging. This goes on and goes on. From within the gulls mewing. This noise, the void eating it up.

And wild jeweled undertow hauling out the monarch's molten gold from inside elaborate wings through green-black bull kelp of Wednesday on curved root-fill planetary roaring . . . The waves boom, thundering, plastering, and do not work all day until they forget who they are.

The depths break into the rocks. And then it's how quiet the sand's choir can be. It might be the planet seen through our eyes still off in space, still landing near the earth's water, where a boy's fire is a man for the sun's sky.

Guided through days of raw starlight and long throws of liquid floors taken over by light at the edge of the water, the ocean's vast call returns. And the immensity nobody could have invented is forever.

# REPORT ON SOME OF THE FUEL

This heaviness inside us is the scent of marble, the morning light in a Baptist room a mother knew, in the scent of dust kept in a place for weeks. The squirrel waits at the bottom of one of his huge cottonwoods, at the edge of his home, where he can still be wild.

And what is it flaring up into you, through the scent in alleys, from old rooms holding off or flying over our heads in the sleep-roads? What is it flaring up heavily and useably, like veins of coal we are burning?

Like your grandfather, you sit down in the morning before the news comes and stand in a room broken from most of the time being made in the cities. Our teaching comes through chords bodies sound like, and each door they open, with light in the leaves, light in the trunks of maples, in the bones the rock holds as our future.

What is it?—that trees carry the rock like an ancient sailing ship, that we live most wildly off the wave that carries us, in the touch of someone's face? What is it as morning curves back over the car and ra-dio, through merely the brown and gray-brown feathers of a sparrow's wings, and the quickness he takes from us, and gives, in the tender light?

# FLASH OF A DRAGONFLY

In the space a dragonfly enters,
sunlight instantly forms,
as the forest shapes its nest

of dense flowerings, penetrating
what enters us, animal calls
we used to be, that our bodies

remember, and the grandfathers
our bodies remember, and mothers
of the stars we remember, and milk-

voiced aortic violet drifting,
with filaments of stone buildings
from an old world breathing out

of the floors and single walls
as we speak, loosening the wood's
chant, or a riverous sway

of skirts broken from a hawk's
drifting toward another ground
in the air, where it will hover,

the way our bodies lift us
through the surface as we move
or sit, mountain air offshore

through slanted light of weekday
hours of training that harden
a steel pipe, like the chestnut

scent in a friend's long hair,
or the fragile minutes a mother
gives month after month

to the new one, his spine
a luminous electric sapling
in cottonwoods and uncut grasses,

the dragonfly darting ahead
of daylight, his bonelit radium
flash calling deep in the day.

# AWAKE AT NIGHT

The night sleeps and wakes in its spiralling spines of stars,
and planets dip into the waters
that flow them and rock them,
as night glows from a Ford, from a trumpet
deep in the numbers, from folded sheets
in a closet back in prehensile chords.
The moon's dark self is a shadow in sentences,
with its dark root in the ground
before anything sees anything, much less thinks
of the night rolling up through the valley in the engine block,
the black of interstellar Tibetan chanting not done,
the shifting of horses in stalls that do not form,
the blast furnace baking the diamond question
before it is asked, before anything is known.
It is the night returning, taking away the rust of noise
and the taste of rice fried with ginger,
holding things so deeply they do not exist
in a past or future forever the small business
nowhere and nothing but night between things,
night in front of and behind things, ushering
down the long chambers of turning atoms and stars.

**

Night breaks open in the orange blossoms
and blasts through the spectrums making a light,
making lights on tables, the current running
through the walls from the dark, volcanic and ancient,
churning up the visible world inside its heart
of still calm, but before there was calm, before
there was this. Night unfolds. A light
in the hallway shows where to walk
back to the bedroom of silence and air
moving and night unfolding open again
into dreams and closing its petals then,
and pulsing open into the dreams

70

and closing back into the bud,
into the seed, into its solidness,
empty, vibrating, suddenly
as if nothing further had been
what we were seeking so mindfully.

# THE UNANSWERING WILL GO UNANSWERING

A wall that stands there in space.
A noise of a hummingbird's wings.
Red cliffs back in the foothills
    that read like inside chanting.
The mastodon sides and flanks
     and faces of some rocks.
A different red in the skin of peaches,
     a purple at the edges of a place with no buildings.
And wings that hear us with our spines,
     light that flows from inside the galaxy.
A green fire from the seed reaching into its hope.
A wall as sun comes down around it,
    and through it, to its home.
A wall with rain forest grown up around it.
A surge in the arms of someone who holds you.
The new blueberries, squirrels, mushroom,
     or wooden table.
A quick city and long nights of the sky.
A hornet flying some of the meat away.

# IN THE SANCTUARY OF FORGETTING

Like a world blessed by ether fragrant with fresh mint
of the root hum, like a vagrant episode beside himself
in an alley of himself.  Like a dolphin trained to the tines
of a vibrating sitar of waters, each shuddering living
molecule rooted on its fork of pre-tonal tuned silence.

Like a man giving away his suitcoat, the Amazonian moth
crawls out of its old body stuck to a tree, and the tree
flies with the moth through the night when the man learns
how much of the tree the world is, flying off so often.

And like a cat whose mansion is a wild field a voice roams
in a single word like *crow*, like *onion*, like *brotherhood*,
felt in the shoulders and flanks of the bodily ancient road
through whose bones our bones grow blood of the apples,
through whose crow our crow rolls bread in the stones,
in the scent of mushroomy fir dirt and pungent pitch,
in the shaking of dried cornstalks buried in the ear.

Like an eye a dolphin carries as her own, back to a source
of water.  Like a love root the tree holds over the valley,
like a building reaching back into the unknown dream place
or a woman pumping her muscles into a machine of health
at the club, the world is blessed by more than it knows
and everything is more than it seems, and bodies work

by how they are more than could ever be seen or summed up.
Like a storm of snow that falls around the inside light.
Like a dusk that heals and fragrant blackberry ground.
Like a milk drinking its flights of moths into the pulse
of the color green, there is walking, in the root hum.
There is licorice, cardamom, ancient health the body now
builds on, finding itself through the self of the root hum.

# IN THE MIND AND SKY

Downtown the punch press churns in its oil, repeating itself,
and grandmother melts the butter, as slender minerals spark up
in the stove light, the sound of breathing light, apples

forming over the eaves of houses, the boy hearing his mother's
breath when he looks at a locust shell on the boxelder trunk.
He turns around—was it his breath, or the trees and grass?

Then there are years, infrared weeks, sometimes a rider coming
this way on the southern cross of Asian wind chime villages,
in gusts so long held out into the abyss they shatter and form,

his wartime, his looking for work, the underwater black-white
reddened negatives, sometimes jazz or Hendrix playing it out
into all unity-fission, full passion, or he slows back, into

emerald of mind, the pungency of plants and faint scent of hair,
with snow falling from a first time he remembers, in daylight,
forest-lit, that dream-day Saturday, the downtown sway of ships

as he saw them before waking once, and the other dreams that spoke.
He knows waves of first light when everything is seen again,
the chestnut trees in Portland one broken afternoon in a thousand

blossoms, in the sun, the sun floating on constant space, formed
from solar matter, packing cliffs with stone faces and webbed
in jewels mumbling from ocean floors through the weeks, with

blue afternoons where the elk turns in the antlers of forest breath
and wind and those he now fills and turns, carrying, with solid
night floating on impulse, a boy hearing his mother's breath.

# A DREAM OF THE HORSE

(a report)

In a dream that woke me the other night
a horse I was familiar with was extremely happy.
We stood in front of an old school on a warm day,
and the horse rolled onto his back like a dog,
loving the way the afternoon grass feels
and sunlight holds and gives us a place.

It was the horse I had been trusting
to find his way back home in the dark
of the previous night, perhaps, or the carrier
of some of the weight of my trying to get somewhere
through the terrains of what I have learned.
His happiness filled him and came to me.

He rolled on the ground and became a gorilla
suddenly. I scratched and petted his head,
and he was even more happy. I looked at him,
trying to understand, but there was no mistake.
He was just here, nothing to carry, his back
on the earth. We had made it into our lives.

# SHOWER

I know there is so much working
into itself, becoming
what it was, moving on
and staying, heavy
with workweeks and gravity.
But then I saw the bar of soap
and thought of the love it gives.
First, rainwater is pumped
beneath people talking
or sleeping in rooms they paint
orange or blue in a dream,
where they find hummingbirds
by the window, say 2,
then 9, and then the backyard
has so many hummingbirds
hovering and diving down
into suddenly appearing
crimson blossoms. So the water
is piped beneath that, into
the house and tank where it waits,
loosening, heating up,
over astral blue flames
that also come from the ground.
When the shower is started,
the water falls and soon begins
steaming.  A person steps in
and stands under the rain
from weeks ago, and under
steaming drops roots gave off
and trees shook out of the wind.
But then the soap radiates
and floats into a hand,
and swims around
on so much soft skin
like a lover who kisses
his lover everywhere

his lips go.  Every touch
slides and loosens in the foam
and cream that is scented
a little gingery and musky,
but like rain falling
in a fine mist in summer,
after a swim in the ocean,
and there is nothing else
to do but feel the water
waking the water
deep in the body,
lifting it.

# SANDBAGGING THE BANKS

Sandbagging the banks of oblivion,
using our best science and historical data,
summoning up explorers of distant survival
and the strongest thick-trunked cottonwoods
full of river rains and luminous August dust
vibrating how the winds breathe in subatomics,
pulsing with bulldozers through flattened canyons
of news talk, we were doing our level best
in spite of the predictions that everything
we know and everyone we love will vanish
in crystalline outer-space midnight eventually.

That ought to be enough, you'd think, to bring
back the desire to live in the only hour
we have here, but still many work against
neighbors, trying to carve some sheer trophy
out of the money radios flooding our houses
with suggestions demanding material form.
Nobody wants to vanish, no people or dogs,
no houses or fir trees, and so the sandbagging
with neon signs and pleasure crafts traveling
rivers of personal intrigue have continued
rising out of the mud into the landscapes,
and lace has been held out against the candlelight,
workboots have followed their iron stairways,
instruction books have blown open like car doors,
as dogs have been barking and no one wants to vanish.

Clearly, no one wants to swell and explode into sky
and rain, and no one wants to fall out of body
into star-swirled ditches of a billion miles forever
curving back around what it was signalling,
and no one wants to be mud on the feet of the dog
or glowing paint on the side of a lost bridge.
No one wants to walk out in a body and never return.
No one wants to see what they've worked toward

swept up in a broth of tonnage and continuum,
the sparking wires traveling behind the theater
sliding down the collapsing cliff into the muddy river,
the plutonium burning floors and walls from inside
molecules, the river inside the molecules
overflowing with thick nothing, with absence
of whatever this was, and nobody knows
what to expect really, past a certain point.

# THE NEXT LIGHT

The next light that forms in the galaxy,
in its waver, reaching here, where the river
turns back into its waves and glistens
over the rocks, miles from the business . . .

And the wheels of the stars break
down into stars that appear, and potential
flares in the first waves and pulls back
into the people we became or come up to.

Deep in the yards and the fields and miles
and the turns, the earth of wheels breaks
through its covers and minds of the hour,
where day spirals in work of the seeds.

The sun becomes what it fills, and forms
in the tiniest being that might hinge
her breath on the charge of a plant,
or on an animal's call as the moon lands.

A city that knows her name lumbers heavily,
like an earth father who learns with the snow
and lights that the one asking is part
of the dawn, in a field of scattered dawns.

# THREE WITH THE SUN

I. *Is the Light Breathing?*

It's in the corn stands, the night wheat, the sassafras lingering, in radio-hazed A-flats combing scarlet porches, the floors of stone, shouldering underground aortic forests.

It's in the street-worn slips and twigs and panthery apricot lattice around the hotel, the one hundred things speaking in a thing, the bombshelters where school children walk lugging green lanterns. Or in multiplied birds, multiplied hair, a bend in the taste of peaches, faintly pitched with root resin, the crackling uncontrolled mica and whole largely unseen clusters of Tibetan quartz.

It's in kneeling by the bed, the curve of cheekbones, the hot membery minute out of focus then back at once in an arc of electrical sumac, the green salt in the green melons, 6 p.m. loose in a small thing speaking for another thing, near the feathery etchings.

Is the light breathing? Is the space the light finds breathing? Is the violet haze poured back under the house slow enough? The turtle's lungs, the rugged turtle face saying something in grooves and hollows, back in, with another north, with other speeds, saying what? Say this far back into next century's past. Say it will be all right.

II. *On the Edge of Form*

How could this place happen like this? Not so far from the rac-
coon teaching her babies back in the indigo blackberry. The river always
itself, not so far from the white moth, the warm mint tassels near a be-
ginning. Not far from the horse chewing a candlelight of hay back into
her body. A crescent moon lit over a first ocean.

In space, in the center, roaring with vacuum and form, planets
wheeling the churning suns around in coves, with a blue jay near the fac-
tory blue, with purple underlight, the elephant's mothering contrabass for
miles from where we took her. Not far from soot billowing through
1932 in the color red. Not far off from cool water of sleep, overflow-
ing banks, the matter making up glowing matter. Say it will be all right.

III. *When So Much Is Happening with the Quiet*

Violet pours through the grasses. Mirrors honey the phone booth plutonium back in Rexall's, near the trophy of liberty. Red distant flares pomegranate open, busty Far West Federal flying its chariot showroom, the landlord changing our minds, plumbing flying through rich dusk looking for houses, ancestors out of focus in the focused wave of a twenty-year stretch.

Who was it who dreamt around us, stopping mid-air, the pelicans rushing a few feet over the water, the red-rooted galaxy rain protoplasmic, cardinal, echoing money sold before a person touches it, the slamming of a van door touching the lake absently, down to a turtle, the dog's eyes of the sky seeing itself, the broccoli's soul tower?

For a while the photon street lagoons, eucalyptus groves in photon business, for a while Monday's thundermass infrared with animal dreams, the black soil of light making black soil, for a while the Bengali cloth, for a while the guitar spirit. The rings buried miles under the ways things are. The bones surfacing, then plunging down into dark and then rising up in our bones, then dissolving. The dusk through buildings, igniting the windows. For a while then the ducks shouting to one another at 11:00 p.m. under the nearby sky. Say it will be all right.

# ROOMS LIT FROM THE REACHES

Bless the surge in spools of urgency,
citrus in the mouth of a kiss, silicone
of research, sister of the cool alfalfa.
Take the electricity into cities of cells,
and ring the wood, wrap lives within lives
as you have done, wisdom before thinking.
Bless the generals with specifics reached
by their overview, shieldbug on the screen,
footprint from the ant, lamp lit by water
in a river, table solid from its lost leaves.
Bless the strong arms of laws lanterned
by mushrooms in culverts of the fallen
unheard-of logs where ferns lift slightly
all conditions, even downtown in the hotel.
Bless the primordial screak of metal warped down,
rust of given blood, spores that puff through
air with microscopic galaxies and the blue hum.

**

Bless the egg with a salmon swimming to leave it.
Bless the question with rain cupped in the root-curved
asking, where the possum grubbed in possumy violet,
where the green fly woke like a pound of uranium,
in the reaches, bless us, mother of the sun.

Bless the shrine with a roof over the man's head,
and bless the tank with chili in emergency shelters,
and take us back, orange-throated robin's call,
sonic firs, uncles of space, hands of the boy
inside us, torch-lit caves inside us.

Father of ground, hone our root steps.
Reddening apples, bless the roundness,
mother of space, whose long hair is sound,
whose letting go holds, mother of the sun.

# ALL THIS IS MODIFIED

All this is modified by the trains
and the lightness of hair.

It is modified by flute music
in the Peruvian mountain town.

It is a canyon breathing with grain,
as a new hive swirls on the edge.

It is rocked by sparrows, by leaf masks
and forest lungs, and blue sky in the sky.

It is turned with old glass doorknobs
and a nuclear war that didn't happen.

And inside the body, inside the bread,
huge sunflowers bow, luminous, in August.

All this is modified by the falling
center of the falling world of an apple.

And the wild curry reaches an unborn doctor,
with African metal bells shaking infinity.

And whatever is privately owned
is also owned by the afternoon rain.

And the kiss on the infant's belly
returns to him many years later.

# About the Author

James Grabill's *Poem Rising Out of the Earth and Standing Up in Someone* (Lynx House Press, 1994) was awarded the Oregon Book Award for Poetry in 1995. Other books include *Through the Green Fire* (Holy Cow! Press, 1995), which was a finalist for the Oregon Book Award for Literary Nonfiction in 1995; *In the Coiled Light* (NRG, 1985); *To Other Beings* (Lynx House Press, 1981); and *Clouds Blowing Away* (kayak & Seizure Books, 1975). His poems have appeared widely in such magazines as *kayak*, *New Letters*, *Willow Springs*, *Caliban*, *Poetry East*, *Poetry Northwest*, *East West Journal*, and many others. Presently, Grabill lives in Portland, Oregon, and teaches at Clackamas Community College in Oregon City. He grew up in Bowling Green, Ohio, in the Eisenhower, Kennedy, and Johnson years.